IN MY HEAD

A new play

by Chris Mayo

Published by Playdead Press 2015

© Chris Mayo 2015

Chris Mayo has asserted his rights under the
Copyright, Design and Patents Act, 1988, to be
identified as the author of this work.

A CIP catalogue record for this book is available from
the British Library.

ISBN 978-1-910067-39-0

Playdead Press
www.playdeadpress.com

Cuckoo Bang Present

IN MY HEAD
A NEW PLAY BY CHRIS MAYO

First performed at The Proud Archivist, London on 9th November 2015 with the following cast and crew:

Matt Lim
Louise Trigg
Paul Huntley-Thomas
Elin Doyle
Holly Mallett
Dan Burman

Director **Chris Mayo**
Assistant Director **Joe Boylan**
Sound Designer **Misha Anker**
Stage Manager **Michaela Cervenakova**
Produced by **Cuckoo Bang**

Very special thanks to
The Peter De Haan Charitable Trust, Jill Ruddock, Peter & Angela Nicklin, Kathleen Nicklin, Andrew Nicklin, Andy Cormack, Mike & Sylvia Mayo, Julie Burman, Peggy King, Mary Mallett, Chris Harvey, Rachel Burnham, Tim Dingle, Poppy Hillstead, Hector Proud, The Proud Archivist, Jake Orr, Theatre Delicatessen, Dani Mansfield and all our wonderful Kickstarter donators who made this production possible.

CUCKOO BANG

Cuckoo Bang was formed by Chris Mayo in October 2012 as a platform to showcase emerging creative talent, their first play *Between Ten and Six* was performed at The Etc. Theatre (October 2012), Leicester Square Theatre (April 2013) and Brighton Fringe (May 2013). In January 2015 the company was joined by co-artistic director Holly Mallett and work began on *In My Head* which had development workshops at Theatre Royal Stratford East in April 2015 and its first public performance on the 9th November 2015 at The Proud Archivist in East London. Aside from productions Cuckoo Bang regularly hold workshops and networking events for emerging creatives, most recently *Deli Meets* in partnership with A Younger Theatre, The Human Zoo Theatre Company and Theatre Delicatessen.

www.cuckoobang.co.uk / @cuckoobang

CHRIS MAYO
Writer / Director

Chris Mayo is an actor, writer, comedian and founder of Cuckoo Bang. Performing credits include: *Romeo & Juliet* (The Nuffield Theatre), *Between Ten And Six* (The Etc Theatre, Leicester Square Theatre, Brighton Fringe), *Eastenders* (BBC), *Chris Mayo's Identity Crisis* (Leicester Comedy Festival, Brighton Fringe, Edinburgh Fringe) and various UK and international commercials. *In My Head* is his second published play as a playwright and his directorial debut.

JOE BOYLAN
Assistant Director

Joe is a theatre-maker, director and a founding member of Barrel Organ Theatre Company. He trained in France at Ecole Philippe Gaulier and makes work that attempts to bridge the worlds of theatre, clown, mask, puppetry and more contemporary UK performance practices. Recent work includes *Some People Talk About Violence* (Barrel Organ, Summerhall, Camden Peoples Theatre), *The Gods of Pick 'n' Mix* (Sad Siren Theatre, Sheffield Theatre Deli), *Black Dog Gold Fish* (Parrot in the Tank, Vaults Festival) and *(I feel fine)* (Fat Git Theatre, Vaults Festival).

MISHA ANKER
Sound Designer

Misha studied at the Royal Central School of Speech and Drama, graduating with a 2.1 in theatre sound. She has been working in theatre since 2011 and *In My Head* is her second show with Cuckoo Bang.

MICHAELA CERVENAKOVA
Stage Manager

Michaela graduated from the Royal Central School of Speech and Drama and is now working as a freelancer in stage management and events production. Work credits include: *The Immigrant* (Joy Garoro-Akpojotor / Rich Mix), *Black Dog Gold Fish* (Parrot in The Tank / The Vaults), *My Girl 2* (Dilated Theatre Company / Old Red Lion Theatre) and *Bratislava Design Week*.

MATT LIM
Richard / Steve / Mike / Various

Since graduating from the University of Cambridge, Matt has enjoyed numerous success on stage and screen, credits include: *Blood Wedding* (Barons Court Theatre) and *2 Complicated* (Brighton Fringe & Barons Court Theatre). He is also a multi award-nominated writer and director, and has written for the Cambridge Footlights and Newsrevue in recent years.

LOUISE TRIGG
Stacey / Kelly / Nurse / Various

Louise trained at East 15 Acting School. Theatre credits include *Bunco & Cleavdon Road* (Temporary Theatre Company), *Fake Fur Coat* (Pensive Federation), *Humans Inc.* (The Alchemist). Voice Over work includes Anxiety UK helpline.

PAUL HUNTLEY-THOMAS
Gameshow Host / Man / Graduate / Various

Paul graduated with a degree in Performance Art from De

Montfort University. He has since performed for a number of theatre companies across the country in productions ranging from street theatre to appearing at the Royal Albert Hall. He has toured internationally with a number of Shakespeare plays, has appeared in a wide variety of short films and has just shot a series for satellite TV.

ELIN DOYLE
Carol / Woman / Doctor / Contestant / Various

After a career as a foreign currency dealer, Elin returned to acting and graduated from Rose Bruford College in 2013. Credits include The Woman in Simon Stephens' *Pornography* and a European tour of *The Elephant Man*. She recently appeared as Scapin in an original French version of Molière's classic comedy, *Les Fourberies de Scapin*. Elin lived in Nice, France for several years and speaks fluent French.

HOLLY MALLETT
Sarah / Girl / Businesswoman / Contestant / Various

A graduate of East 15, Holly balances her time between acting and music. A professional drummer, Holly has played for a number of artists and companies including Universal Music and a residency as RARE Productions in-house drummer. Acting credits include: NSDF award-winning *League of St George* (The Hope Theatre), *London Jungle Book* (National Theatre Workshop), *CBeebies Live!* (Arena Tour) and *Shakespeare For Breakfast* (Edinburgh Fringe). Holly is an improv performer and company manager for *Waiting For The Call* and is co-artistic director of *Cuckoo Bang*.

DAN BURMAN
Martin / Businessman / Graduate / Various

Dan trained at East 15 Acting School. Theatre credits include Eledor in *The Never Ever Cafe* (XO Theatre) and Nick Pickle in *Long Live The Ringmaster* (Kinetix Theatre Company). Film credits include Matthew Grey in *I'm Still Here* and Dean in *In Circles*. Dan is also a highly experienced fight co-ordinator for film, television and stage.

Author's notes

The play is intended for a cast of 6 to play multiple roles, however it could easily be much larger or smaller.

With the exception of those that are numbered, scenes can be performed in any order.

Gender, age, character names, locations and other details are often left deliberately vague to allow for different casting and staging interpretations.

The following text was correct at the time of starting rehearsals but may vary from the final production.

Onstage are six perspex boxes brightly lit from within,

There is a slight haze onstage. The setting is non specific.

The cast are sat on top of the boxes as the audience enter.

Lights fade to black, we are in total darkness except for the light of the perspex boxes.

A busy hustle and bustle of characters, snippets of scenes to come & projections.

The noise builds into a frenzy and then everything is suddenly silent.

FUCK BUDDIES

GIRL	So...what? Fuck buddies?
GUY	Huh?
GIRL	We've got to talk about this sometime, we can't just...
GUY	Yeah, alright, I know.

Pause.

GIRL	Like, now.
GUY	Ok, yeah, but no... I hate that word.
GIRL	What?
GUY	"Buddy", sounds so American, so arrogant. "Hey buddy, d'you want me to wank you off?"
GIRL	What was that?
GUY	An American.
GIRL	Which American?

GUY	I don't know, what do you mean "which American"? A non specific one...
GIRL	Why is a non specific American offering to wank you off?
GUY	He's not! It was... Jesus are you always going to be like this?
GIRL	Are you trying to tell me something Mark? You don't want us to be fuck buddies because you'd rather imagine non specific American men wanking you off?
GUY	Not fuck buddies and...
GIRL	What's he wanking you off with? A donut? That'd be the ultimate American wank wouldn't it? Mmm
GUY	You're weird, you know that?
GIRL	My ex said I was "kookily cuntish".
GUY	Nice.

Silence.

GIRL	So, ok, so, not fuck buddies.
GUY	Look, we don't need to *be* anything do we? Why does it matter?
GIRL	Well I just want to feel like...
GUY	We have fun.
GIRL	Sometimes.
GUY	We're friends.
GIRL	Yeah.
GUY	Well then.

11

GIRL	Fun friends?
GUY	Fuck me, what is this Cbeebies?
GIRL	Sorry... I'm just trying to make it...
GUY	It's fine.

Pause.

GIRL	I don't want to be needy or pressure you but -
GUY	It's fine.

He kisses her. He drinks some coffee. He re-arranges his clothes.

GUY	I should probably head off.
GIRL	Sex chums?
GUY	[*Laughs*] Wow. You...sex chums? That's a serious proposal is it?
GIRL	Ok, maybe not that but....

He laughs again

GIRL	Well, don't be a prick about it.
GUY	Come on, really? You don't think that's funny? You want me to take 'sex chums' seriously?
GIRL	I'm getting too old for this.
GUY	...How old are you again?
GIRL	Great... exactly my point... "thanks for the fuck, same again next week, if I'm not busy, I might be busy, I'll text you...by the way, what was your name, or, age, or" -

GUY	Sarah, and fuck you, I don't sound like that.
GIRL	Ok, well, well done, you remembered. And I'm 25 for the record, if you want to jot that down, I'm a 25 year old woman, with her own flat, and a decent job, and my looks, I look ok don't I? I mean, I think I do, and I have a personality, which I know doesn't really matter to you right now, but I, I should just be able to at least hold someone down who wants to talk to me and -
GUY	Look, I like you a lot... Sarah... and... you're, you're really you, y'know, I don't think I've ever met anyone else like you but I can't just -
GIRL	Well you did, and you have, several times, four if I remember rightly, no wait, five, five if we count the time you spaffed in your pants and fell asleep.
GUY	I was drunk.
GIRL	We're *always* drunk, that's why this happens. I'm, I'm not a, so... I just need *something* else, I need to -
GUY	I don't think I can give you something else. Probably not. We've been through this, you know the deal, I can't commit to, I can't stay and chat and talk about your "problems" every time we... I don't have time for that.

Pause.

13

GIRL   Ok, no, you're right, sorry I was being
              unreasonable, wanting to, to talk to my...
              whatever you are, about my "problems",
              what a dick.

GUY   Look, It's just, it's always fun, and
              then, this happens, every time, why can't
              things just be simple, y'know, obviously
              you've got some stuff going on, I get that,
              I'm sorry, I hope you get it all sorted out,
              but I don't need someone who's all -

GIRL   What? Someone who's what?

VERBATIM 1

ACTOR 1   People like to look at my life and say that
              X caused Y. That there was a reason for
              my depression and subsequent slide into
              what I term, in polite company, a
              breakdown. The truth is that, for as long
              as I can remember, I've been unhappy.

ACTOR 2   Attempted suicide at 18, 21, 24. I'm alright
              now though.

ACTOR 3   Sometimes I have a pain in my stomach so
              bad that I can't stand up. It's hard to fully
              describe how I feel, it makes me restless, I
              feel on edge, as though I can't sit still.

ACTOR 4   When I'm ill I disappear from the world,
              feel nobody wants me around, that I am
              worth nothing. My marriage was in part
              destroyed by my lack of belief that I could
              be loved. I tell myself it will pass, that the
              thoughts aren't real. It scares me that one

14

day I won't be able to fight the feelings,
and in a moment of weakness I… sorry… I
feel like I should apologise, it's not often I
get to say this stuff but it's like the biggest
weight has been lifted from my shoulders
every time I do.

AD AGENCY

GUY 1   You ready?

*He clicks a clicker and an image of a "mental patient"
appears. A tired looking man in a torn shirt covered in blood.*

GUY 2   Happy fucking Halloween!

GUY 1   You like yeah?

GUY 2   Love it mate, yep, really funny.

GUY 1   We are going to sneak up and fuck those
                   Sainsbury's cunts in the arse with this one.

GUY 2   Taste the difference bitch.

They laugh and high five.

GUY 1   New guy?

He looks unsure.

GUY 1   Uhh, don't like that face.

GUY 3   I dunno, I'm just not… sure.

GUY 1   Come on mate, it's a dead cert, Psycho.
                   Ward. It's current, it's creepy, it's -

GUY 3   Offensive.

GUY 2	It's not offensive mate... not if you've got a fucking brain in your head, it's a costume, name me one offensive costume.
GUY 3	The KKK
GUY 1	Yeah, well, that's like a real thing.
GUY 3	*This* is a real thing.
GUY 1	Yeah, but, like not a history real thing, not the same.
GUY 2	Look, let him do his pitch mate, maybe if he explains it more you'll...
GUY 1	Exactly, appreciate that. Ok, so, picture the scene.

He clicks his fingers. The lights change.

GUY 2	Ooh, nice.
GUY 1	It's Friday night, 31st October, Halloween, everyone's getting ready to go out, dressed up, up for a big one, looking. great. Mark from accounts is the headless man, Dan in IT has come as the corpse of Jimmy Savile.
GUY 2	Zombie paedo, classic.
GUY 1	Kelly, the receptionist, slutty black cat.
GUY 2	100% would... sorry.
GUY 1	And then, there's a slow, heavy, knocking at the door.

Guy 1 knocks.

GUY 1	Jimmy Savile looks at the headless man, the headless man, looks at the Slutty black cat -
GUY 2	What with?
GUY 1	What?
GUY 2	Well he's headless, what's he looking at her with?
GUY 1	He, um, he's not actually headless mate, it's a costume, there's two holes in the fake neck stump for him to peek through.
GUY 2	Right, yep, got it.
GUY 1	Kelly feels a lump in her throat, bit late for trick or treaters she thinks, she's apprehensive, her palms are sweating, she swallows.
GUY 2	Yes she does... yep, inappropriate, fair enough.
GUY 1	She makes her way over to the door, she opens it, and standing there, is a man, he looks just like you or me but something's not quite right, he's in a torn shirt, shivering and covered in blood, no shoes on his feet. "I'm terribly sorry to bother you he says, but I've run out of my medication, I tried the pharmacies around here but they're all closed, I don't suppose anyone in this house has any Flupentixol to tie me over for the weekend? I need it to be... normal again. "Yeah, nice costume mate", says Kelly, good little bit of acting, but you're too late, sorry, we gave away all our

17

sweets and we're off out now, have a good night yeah?". She slams the door in his face, they all laugh "What a fucking loon" says Jimmy Savile. They grab their bags, their coats and then it comes again, the same, slow, knock. "Ok, he's pissing me off now" says Kelly, and she opens the door a second time, "Look, I already told you we don't have any..."...She takes a sharp intake of breath, she coughs, she splutters, she looks down to see the man pull a meat cleaver out from her stomach, blood spurts everywhere and she slumps to the floor. The man wipes the blade across his shirt, looks up at the headless man and Jimmy Savile and says "sorry, I guess I'll try next door then". He slams the door shut and the two men look at the twitching slutty cat on the floor as blood oozes across the varnished wood. "PSYCHO WARD. Because everyones a little bit mental".

He laughs. He flicks the lights back on.

Well... what do you think?

GIRLS 1

The sound of heavy rain and distant thunder.

A makeshift shack in a football field at the back of a housing estate.

A worn out electric lantern flickers.

GIRL 1   Why is it always raining when we come here?

GIRL 2 is texting.

GIRL 1   Stace?

GIRL 2   Eh?

GIRL 1   "Why is it always'...Nothing.

Silence

GIRL 1   Who you texting?

GIRL 2   I'm not.

GIRL 1   Well, fuck off, because you are.

Pause

GIRL 2   I'm… just reading.

GIRL 1   Reading? We're in a hut on a fucking football field, at night, in the pissing rain, I didn't come here to watch you read...

GIRL 2   Alright. Sorry.

Pause.

GIRL 2   You're not going to try and kiss me or something are you?

GIRL 1   What? Ew, no.

GIRL 2   Ok cool, because I thought that might of been a moment, just then, was that a moment?

GIRL 1   It wasn't a moment.

GIRL 2   Cool, because, you know, I love you, as a mate, but, that would just be… nah.

Awkward Pause.

GIRL 1   So... who?

GIRL 2	Huh?
GIRL 1	Texting...who. Are. You. Texting?
GIRL 2	I just said, I'm not texting... I'm reading a... thing... I've finished now anyway.
GIRL 1	Alright.

Pause

GIRL 1	Is everything… ok?
GIRL 2	Yeah, fine, you?
GIRL 1	Yeah.

Beat.

GIRL 1	Well...
GIRL 2	What?
GIRL 1	No, It's... I went to that party on Saturday night.
GIRL 2	Oh fuck, yeah, with Mike, Magic Mike! How was it?
GIRL 1	Great.
GIRL 2	Yeah?
GIRL 1	Yeah, you should have come it was, fun.
GIRL 2	Nah.
GIRL 1	Why not? There were loads of people from school there.
GIRL 2	Exactly, people are dicks.
GIRL 1	Not all people.

GIRL 2	Most people, most people are, statistically, dicks.
GIRL 1	Mike isn't.
GIRL 2	Yeah well that's what he wants you to think isn't it? They're never dicks to start with.
GIRL 1	Mike isn't a dick Stacey.

Pause

GIRL 1	He... has a dick though.

She laughs.

GIRL 2	Oh, shit, you didn't...?
GIRL 1	No! Well yeah, sort of, we did, a bit.
GIRL 2	Oh. My. God, he's what like, 22?
GIRL 1	No, shut up, look you can't tell anyone ok?
GIRL 2	Alright.
GIRL 1	Thanks.

Pause.

GIRL 2	What do you mean exactly...a bit?
GIRL 1	Well... we just like...

She badly mimes giving a blowjob. Girl 2 looks confused.

GIRL 2	You brushed his teeth?
GIRL 1	What? Shut up, you know what I mean.
GIRL 2	Yeah, no, what?
GIRL 1	A blow job.

GIRL 2	Oh God, that's rank, you don't where it's been, why would anyone want to... that increases your risk of cancer you know, not to mention the fact it's horrific.
GIRL 1	Cancer?
GIRL 2	Yeah, putting... willies... in your...
GIRL 1	You did not just say willies, oh my god that is so embarrassing.
GIRL 2	What's wrong with willies?
GIRL 1	Stop saying it! It's dicks... or cocks... or... God.
GIRL 2	Well, doing that... it increases your risk of cancer.
GIRL 1	Well, he doesn't have cancer so...you need to stop reading so much, it fucks with your head.
GIRL 2	My head's already fucked.
GIRL 1	Huh?
GIRL 2	Doesn't matter, I'm just...
GIRL 1	What?
GIRL 2	Sorry....
GIRL 1	Are you sure you're alright, you just fucking trailed off there.
GIRL 2	Yeah, no, yeah, I've just not been getting much sleep that's all.
GIRL 1	Ok, d'you want to head back?
GIRL 2	No.

Sudden burst of thunder and more rain.

GIRL 1   Fuck. I don't like it in here when it's like this, doesn't feel... safe, it's creepy.

GIRL 2   What you worried about? It's just rain.

GIRL 1   I know, but, it's dark.

GIRL 2   Aww babe.

GIRL 1   Piss off.

GIRL 2   We've got our trusty lamp. We'll be alright.

Pause.

GIRL 2   So, what was it... like?

GIRL 1   Well, his name is "Magic Mike" Stace, it was...

GIRL 2   Magic?

GIRL 1   It was alright. Smelt funny.

GIRL 2   Shit.

GIRL 1   Tasted worse.

GIRL 2   God, why would anyone want to...

GIRL 1   Like a Dairylea triangle left out in the Sun.

GIRL 2   Right, shut up, I'm gagging.

GIRL 1   I was gagging.

She mimes choking on a dick.

GIRL 2   You are literally the worst person I have ever met.

They both laugh.

GIRL 2	Why would anyone leave a dairylea triangle in the Sun?
GIRL 1	I dunno, an abandoned picnic? You think too much.
GIRL 2	Maybe.

Pause.

GIRL 1	You know you can talk to me right?
GIRL 2	We are talking.
GIRL 1	You know what I mean, I know something's up, I'm not stupid.

Pause.

GIRL 2	You'd run.
GIRL 1	Wouldn't.
GIRL 2	You would, if I told you, showed you, honestly, you'd fuck right off.
GIRL 1	Well, maybe if you've like killed someone or something, then I'd run, really fucking fast, just for my own protection... but I'd still text you... fuck, have you killed someone? Have you brought a body here? Are you going to kill me?
GIRL 2	I haven't killed anyone.
GIRL 1	Oh, ok, well then we're cool.

Pause.

GIRL 1 takes off her hoody. She has cut marks across her arms and stomach, some fresh.

GIRL 1	Shit.

COME OUT?

A man is stood centre stage, he is listening to his voicemails.

ANSWERPHONE V/O   You have 3 new messages. To listen to your messages press 1. First new message, received Thursday at 2.45pm

GIRL V/O   Hey Rich, it's me, haven't heard from you in a while just wondered if you fancied a drink? Give me a call when you've got a moment? Alright, bye.

ANSWERPHONE V/O   To listen to the message again press 1, to save the message press 2, to delete the message... message deleted. You have two new messages. Message received, Friday, at 6.31pm.

GUY V/O   Hey man, it's Dan, oh that rhymed, dick-head. Yeah, so, me and the guys from work were wondering how you were getting on? Heard you were a bit sick or something? Hope it's not the shits. Give us a bell for a beer or something. Alright, later dude.

ANSWERPHONE V/O   To listen to the message agai... message deleted. You have one new message, new message received today at 11.35am.

CAROL V/O   Hi Richard, it's Carol, just confirming we're meeting at 1.30pm tomorrow, if I don't hear otherwise, I'll assume all is well, any problems do give me a call. Bye for now.

ANSWERPHONE V/O To listen to the message... received today at 11.35am. Hi Richard, it's Carol, just confirming we're meeting at 1.30pm tomorrow, if I don't hear otherwise, I'll assume all is well, any problems do give me a call. Bye for now. To listen to message again... your message will be saved for 7 days. End of messages.

AD AGENCY 2

GUY 1   So -

He flicks through a file.

Stephen. What the fuck was that?

GUY 3   Sorry?

GUY 2   This morning, in the meeting, the costume, you've got a problem with it?

GUY 3   Oh, look, I'm really sorry about that, I just thought it was –

GUY 1   Yeah, ok, look, you've been with us a month now right?

GUY 3   About that, yes.

GUY 2   Bit soon to be chipping in with your opinions at board meeting perhaps?

26

GUY 3   Sorry, when you said you wanted me to give feedback, I thought...

GUY 1   Yeah, we all want feedback mate, but not negative stuff, that's no help is it? We're not expecting you to suck our cocks but you could at least massage our balls a little.

GUY 2   How would you say you're... settling in... generally?

GUY 3   Good yeah.

GUY 1   Comfortable in the office?

GUY 3   Yeah, everyone's very... it's been fine, I haven't really had the chance to...

GUY 2   Look... you and I... and more importantly him (*Gestures to Guy 1*) know that this isn't just about this morning, we've been looking at your figures and party goods should sell mate, that's why you're here to sell more things and make us more money, they've always sold and your figures well, they're not pretty.

GUY 3   Oh.

GUY 1   Yeah, really fucking ugly figures Steve.

GUY 3   I'm sorry if...

GUY 1   We're a multi-billion pound company mate, in one of the biggest industries in the world, we rely on our employees to be the absolute best, without that, we're nothing.

Pause.

GUY 2	So why should we keep you on?
GUY 3	You're firing me?
GUY 1	Didn't say that.
GUY 2	Definitely didn't say that, we're giving you a chance to sell yourself Steve, to fight, so... ding ding.

Pause.

GUY 3	Ok, I... feel that, with my skills, I can offer a fresh and unique approach to...
GUY 1	Yeah, look, fuck that, that's, what, you've prepared that right?
GUY 3	Sorry?
GUY 2	That... speech. You were ready for this weren't you? Had a bad feeling about the email so you wrote something down.
GUY 3	Sorry... I'm not very –
GUY 1	Oh, not is NOT a word we like to use. Positivity is productivity is –
GUY 2	Why do you *need* this job? Be honest.

Pause.

GUY 3	Well, I was off work for 3 months at the beginning of the year and... my family.
GUY 2	Ah ok, now we're getting somewhere. Family man, that's nice.
GUY 1	3 months though? Doesn't sound great, what happened?

GUY 3	I... had a disagreement with my previous employer, about... an... ongoing... medical problem.
GUY 1	That's a shame... let me tell you something; our main priority, after the figures of course, is employee loyalty.
GUY 2	That's not an official motto but it is *fucking* true. What we're trying to say is that we're good people Steve, we understand life sometimes, it gets a bit tough. You need support, but you've got to meet us half way mate.
GUY 3	Yes.
Pause.	
GUY 1	It's not terminal is it?
GUY 3	Terminal? God no, well I *hope*... it's more...
GUY 1	Chronic? They say that can often be just as bad.
GUY 3	No... well, it's nothing really. Nothing that'll stop me from working.
GUY 2	But your previous boss...
GUY 3	Didn't understand. I couldn't get the support...
GUY 2	Sorry to hear that. Really.
GUY 1	So, what... drugs?
GUY 3	No.
GUY 2	Drink?
GUY 1	Technically a drug.

GUY 3	No, I, I'm depressed.
Pause	
GUY 1	Oh... right ok... I see... It's just these... figures Steve, the figures aren't great.

Some mime talking. They shake hands and exit.

PANIC ATTACK

A non specific setting. The scene plays out like a panic attack in terms of pace, rhythm and movement.

/ - Indicates an overlap in the text and where the next line of dialogue starts.

ACTOR 1	It's a tightening of the chest, difficulty breathing and uncontrollable crying.
ACTOR 2	You're trying to wake up but you fall back paralysed with your eyes in the back of your head desperately trying to get a foot hold in reality before you're / sucked under.
ACTOR 1	It's hard to know when it's stopped or if it even / has.
ACTOR 3	Trapped / secluded.
ACTOR 1	I was crying literally all / night for days.
ACTOR 2	Angry at nothing, then angry at / everything.
ACTOR 3	It's a tightening / of the chest,
ACTOR 4	Angry / at...
DOCTOR 1	I'm going to try you on / Citalopram.

30

ACTOR 2	Citalopram, 20mg once a day.
ACTOR 1	It's hard to know when it's stopped.
ACTOR 4	A complete nervous / breakdown.
DOCTOR 2	Have you / tried CBT?
ACTOR 2	Tried CBT. Didn't work.
ACTOR 3	Seroxat 20mg.
DOCTOR 1	Seroxat / 20mg.
ACTOR 4	It speaks to you / in your own voice.
ACTOR 2	In your own / voice.
ACTOR 3	Citalopram 40mg / once a day.
DOCTOR 1	40 mg / once a day.
DOCTOR 2	40mg.
ACTOR 2	Tightening in the / chest, like a heart attack.
ACTOR 1	Chest, like a heart / attack -
ACTOR 3	Keep telling myself / it will pass.
DOCTOR	/ It will pass.
ACTOR 2	But it isn't.
ACTOR 1	Speaks to you in your / own voice.
ACTOR 4	Insomnia and eating problems.
DOCTOR 1	Beta / Blockers.
ACTOR 2	Beta Blockers /
ACTOR 4	CBT.
ACTOR 1	Tightening.

Actors becoming more frantic, loud and distressed.

ACTOR 3   20mg, / 30mg, 40mg.

DOCTOR 2   30mg, 40mg, once a day.

ACTOR 2   In the / chest.

DOCTOR 1   30mg /

ACTOR 4   30mg, 40mg / 50mg.

ACTOR 1   50mg / 60mg.

ACTOR 2   60mg, one a day.

DOCTOR 2   Fluoextine 60mg / once a day.

ACTOR 1   Once a day.

ACTOR 4   Citalopram / 60mg (Made me suicidal).

ACTOR 2   Suicidal

DOCTOR 2   There are possible side / effects.

ACTOR 1   Side / effects?

ACTOR 2   Side effects.

ACTOR 4   / Dizziness.

DOCTOR 2   Dizziness.

ACTOR 2   Bi-Polar Disorder.

ACTOR 1   60mg, tightening in the /

ACTOR 3   Makes the problem worse / before it's better.

ACTOR 1   In the chest.

ACTOR 2   Dry / mouth.

ACTOR 1   Panic.

ACTOR 2   Erratic movement.

DOCTOR 1   / before it's better.

ACTOR 4   Fatigue, Low sex drive.

ACTOR 3   Sex drive?

DOCTOR 2   Tiredness, panic, sleeping / problems.

ACTOR 1   I just don't believe / drugs solve the problem.

ACTOR 4   Drugs solve the problem.

ACTOR 1   CBT.

ACTOR 2   Tired all the time.

ACTOR 3   Prozac, I remember / that one.

ACTOR 4   Efexor 75mg two a day.

ACTOR 1   Twice / a day.

ACTOR 2   20mg.

ACTOR 3   30mg, 40mg.

ACTOR 4   Gin, does gin count?

Beat. Everyone takes a breath.

ACTOR 1   Tightening.

DOCTOR 2   A tightening in the chest.

ACTOR 1   Tightening in / the

ACTOR 3   / the chest.

DOCTOR 1   Dizziness.

ACTOR 1   Uncontrolled movements.

ACTOR 4   60mg, 70mg.

DOCTOR 2	70mg, for 6 months.
ACTOR 2	6 months.
ACTOR 1	12 months.
DOCTOR 1	For 12 months.
ACTOR 2	None worked / long term.
DOCTOR 1	Will work in the long term.
ACTOR 3	Crying all the time.
DOCTOR 2	Fill out this form please.
ACTOR 1	/ this form.
ACTOR 2	/ this form please.
DOCTOR 1	On a scale of 1-10 how severe are your
ACTOR 1	Four, probably a four
ACTOR 3	8.
ACTOR 2	50, 60, 70mg.
ACTOR 4	Tight.
DOCTOR 2	Deep breaths, deep breaths.
ACTOR 1	Deep breaths,

The scene becomes calmer.

ACTOR 2	Deep breaths in.
DOCTORS 1 & 2	Deep breaths in, hold.
ACTOR 1	Hold.
ACTOR 3	Hold.
ACTOR 4	Hold.
ACTOR 2	Hold.

Silence.

DOCTOR 2   And breathe out please.

ACTOR 1   Breathe out.

ACTOR 3   Breathe out.

The actors breathe out.

DOCTOR 1   Good.

DOCTOR 2   Good.

ACTOR 4   Good.

ACTOR 2   Good.

The sounds of calm breathing for a while.

DOCTOR 1   Good.

ACTOR 1   It's, like a tightening in the chest, like a heart attack, but it isn't.

DOCTOR 1   I'm going to prescribe Citalopram, 20mg, once a day. Things will get better.

A collective exhale of breath.

ACTORS

A nightclub. Loud music.

ACTOR 1   Great place.

ACTOR 2   What?

ACTOR 1   GREAT PLACE!

The music softens.

ACTOR 2   Yeah, bit sticky though, fuck, I'm really sweating.

ACTOR 1   It's nice to get out of that room for a bit y'know? Let our hair down.

ACTOR 2   Yeah... It's good though isn't it? I think it's going to be really good.

ACTOR 1   Press night is going to be...

ACTOR 2   Huh?

ACTOR 1   Critics, I'm worried about y'know...

ACTOR 2   Oh fuck, no, seriously, don't even think about... look, we're doing this for us, for our audience, yeah? It's going to be, I think it's going to be really good.

ACTOR 3 enters with drinks.

ACTOR 1   There she is!

ACTOR 3   Sorry, the queue, every other fucking girl was doing the "I've got tits, I'm next" thing. I'm seriously considering getting implants just so I don't have to wait 20 minutes for a fucking jaeger bomb.

ACTOR 2   Might try that myself.

They laugh.

ACTOR 1   Yeah I'd totally fuck you if you were a woman.

ACTOR 2   Oh thanks mate.

ACTOR 1   But thankfully that's never going to happen.

ACTOR 3   Well, it could be worse, at least Martin's spared us his company.

ACTOR 2	God, can you imagine if he'd come? "Where's the fire exit? The music's too loud, I'll just have a water, I hate it, I don't like these people" miserable prick.
ACTOR 1	Come on, he's alright.
ACTOR 2	No, he's awful, he's a fucking awful boring man.
ACTOR 1	He was in Game of Thrones.
ACTOR 2	Yeah, uncredited.
ACTOR 1	Really? I thought he had a -
ACTOR 2	Nope, his agent's sister is fucking the casting director brother. Said can Mike get in on this? Before it was massive you know. He just runs by shouting with a sword or something.
ACTOR 1	Fuck, he really built that up.
ACTOR 2	Exactly. Prick.

PHONE ASSESSMENT

Actor 4 is facing the audience.

MARTIN	7… 8… um, 6, actually 7, yeah 7. Yes, it's high I know that's why I… 8, uh most days I guess… that's, that's most days as well… all days, I feel like that all the fucking time… sorry, yes… how long is this going to take…
NURSE 1	…it's a 10 minute questionnaire, there abouts… we've been speaking for 1 minute now I'd say, so… 9 minutes that's right, no

I can't speak any faster, this is how fast I...
I've been advised to speak at this speed to
ensure all questions are... ok... no that
didn't count towards... we still have 9
minutes left that's right, well... yes... I
need to ask you all the questions to work
out the...the most appropriate treatment
sir... I understand that... yes, so, shall I
continue with the assessment? Thank you.

CALLER 3   ...No medication no, er, not really... well
some weed now and again.

MARTIN   An actor... yes that's my actual job... I'm
rehearsing a play but, nothing really. It can
be... I guess.

CALLER 1   I don't know, 6, 7... no I haven't... no.

MARTIN   I can't say anything, it's, I just can't...
because no-one would fucking employ me
if they knew...

NURSE   I understand you're upset, but if you swear
at me again I'm going to have to terminate
this consultation.

MARTIN   I wasn't... I wasn't swearing at *you*, it's -

CALLER 3   The system, the *wait*, the jumping through
hoops the -

Silence.

NURSE   ...Are you having any thoughts about self-
harm?

CALLER 1   I... I don't know does that bump me up
the list?

NURSE   ...

38

CALLER 1	Sorry, I… No, I haven't.
NURSE	Ok, that's good.
MARTIN	Can I ask you a question?
NURSE	Yes, of course.
CALLERS	Do you think this is fair?
NURSE	Fair?
CALLER 3	Yeah, this process, is it fair?
NURSE	It's… not really my place to say, I just deal with triage consultations.
MARTIN	Oh come on, it's, you know it's not, it took me two weeks just to get this phone call, and then depending on if I give the right or the wrong answers I'll…
NURSE	We are doing all we can.
CALLER 1	Are you?
NURSE	…Yes, we're doing the very best we can

The actors hang up.

NURSE	Hello? Hello?

MARRIED COUPLE

Living room of a council flat. The Man is watching TV. The Woman is obsessively cleaning.

MAN	Sit down.
WOMAN	I will, in a minute.
MAN	They look fine, just leave them alone.

Silence.

MAN   Nothing is going to happen if you just...

WOMAN   In a minute, just watch your TV, please.

Silence.

MAN   Look I can't fucking concentrate, I can't
                   relax with you pottering about.

The woman brings an ornament she is cleaning with her.

Silence.

WOMAN   I'm sorry.

Silence.

The woman continues to scrub the ornament.

Pause. The man watches his wife.

MAN   You ok?

*The woman gives a half smile and nod. Silence. TV sounds.
After a while the man mutes the TV.*

MAN   Is this how you thought we would end up?
                   Like this?

WOMAN   ...Sorry? I...

MAN   We used to love each other... can you
                   remember that? Not just say it, but mean
                   it, really, I would feel it as I said it "I *love*
                   you", and now I just... can you remember
                   feeling like that?

Silence.

MAN   We used to hold hands everywhere we went
                   and kiss each other? Touch, fuck? Not just
                   because we felt we should but because we

40

couldn't do anything else until we had. We needed it, I *needed* you and now it's... we just exist.

Pause.

MAN   Could you even tell me when we last had some sort of fucking connection?

WOMAN   Please don't swear.

Pause.

MAN   Look at you.

WOMAN   I'm fine.

MAN   You're not fine, This isn't a life.

WOMAN   For you, you mean?

MAN   For anyone, we're not alive, I'm married to a woman who's brain is fucked and whose body is...

WOMAN   I'm sorry I ruined your life.

MAN   You just... it makes me *angry*.

WOMAN   I know it does.

MAN   Look I'm just trying to...

WOMAN   You think I like being like this? You think I like being with *you* like this?

MAN   Like you've got a choice.

Silence.

MAN   I've been reading up on it, your condition, there are ways, techniques, medication -

WOMAN   I don't have a "condition"

41

MAN	The Dr said…
WOMAN	The Dr said I was depressed, then the Dr said that I have obsessive tendencies, the Dr said because I scored 40 out of 50 that I should be on medication for a minimum of 12 months to avoid further relapse, The Dr said I should take up pilates, and try a high fibre diet, the Dr knows nothing about me.
MAN	He knows you're not well.
WOMAN	I can't remember what it feels like to be well, I have come to accept the fact that this is the person I am now.
MAN	It's been 2 years!

Pause.

WOMAN	And you want me to forget? Would that make things easier for you?
MAN	I just want you to accept, I want you to move on, I want my wife back.
WOMAN	I want my daughter back.
MAN	I know you…
WOMAN	No, no you don't… you just don't. You couldn't even begin to imagine how I feel… she was taken away from me, and I ache, everything aches, every day, all the time, from when I drag myself out of bed to when I crawl back into it and when I close my eyes, I still see her face, I hear her laugh, I smell her breath, it reminds me of when I was a happy person.

42

A sudden strobing of images. The sounds of two cars colliding. The woman gasps.

WOMAN   I'm terrified to close my eyes, but I do for
             fear that I might forget what she looked
             like. I'm weak and tired because I can't eat,
             but I still cook, because god forbid you
             should have to do something for yourself,
             and when I try and eat with you my
             stomach cramps and I feel like my whole
             body is destroying itself.

She starts to panic, the man goes to help.

MAN   Just calm down, please... fuck... breathe...
             you know this, we've done this.

WOMAN   Don't... touch me... leave... me alone.

MAN   I can't do this, I can't see you like this... I
             can't put myself through... you need to get
             over this.

She takes some deep breaths.

MAN   You need to stop... you need to stop this
             happening... fuck... I deserve better than
             this.

WOMAN   Fuck you.

He thinks for a moment.

MAN   Change your fucking life.

He exits.

RESTAURANT 1

WOMAN   I have to be back by 2.30.

43

MAN	Oh sure, yeah, no, yeah, that's fine.
WOMAN	What was your name again?
MAN	Rich.
WOMAN	Carol.
MAN	Yes, I remember.
WOMAN	So... are you then?
MAN	Sorry?
WOMAN	Rich? I was, making a joke, about your name.
MAN	Oh, ha, middling... average.
WOMAN	I know what middling means.

Awkward silence. Text tone.

WOMAN You don't mind if I?

She gets out her phone.

MAN No no, you... go ahead.

The waiter enters with drinks.

WAITER Your drinks.

He places the drinks on the table.

WOMAN I actually said no ice.

Beat.

WAITER I'm sorry, you did.

The waiter goes to the edge of the stage, take the ice out of the glass and flings it offstage. He walks back to the table, places it down. The man sees this.

WAITER No ice.

The woman is transfixed by her phone.

WOMAN   Thank you.

WAITER   May I take your order?

MAN   Um...

WOMAN   Two minutes.

WAITER   Of course.

The waiter exits.

MAN   You're very good at that.

WOMAN   What?

She continues to text

MAN   Being, authoritative.

WOMAN   It's my job and I really fucking hate ice.
                 I'm cold enough.

MAN   Joke?

WOMAN   No.

MAN   Oh.

She locks her phone.

WOMAN   Yes.

The man laughs awkwardly.

WOMAN   You should change your laugh.

MAN   Oh, ok.

WOMAN   It's not very confident, it's awkward.

MAN   Sorry.

WOMAN   You don't do this very often do you?

MAN	I guess not.
WOMAN	First time?
MAN	3rd.
WOMAN	Fuck. 1 and 2 must have been a hoot.
MAN	Sorry, I...
WOMAN	Stop apologising it's making my vagina fucking seize up.
MAN	...

The waiter walks back to the table.

WOMAN	Two minutes.

The waiter exits.

MAN	We should probably...

Indicates the menu. They both look.

WOMAN	Did you bring one and two here?
MAN	One and? ...Oh yes, um, yeah, yes, I think I did... not together, obviously.
WOMAN	Was that a joke? If it was it wasn't funny. Couldn't you have found somewhere better?
MAN	The food's good.

Pause. The woman looks at the menu.

WOMAN	Probably the chicken.
MAN	Sorry? That wasn't an apology, that was a question.
WOMAN	I'll probably have the chicken.

MAN   Oh right, yes, I'm sure that's good.

The waiter comes back in tentatively.

WOMAN   The chicken.

The waiter scribbles down.

WAITER   The… chicken…

MAN   The pesto and pine nut pasta salad please. No olives… if that's ok

WOMAN   Fuck me

The waiter scribbles. He loudly clicks his pen.

WAITER   Very good.

The waiter exits.

MAN   I'm a vegetarian.

WOMAN   Christ, you really know how to pick them Carol.

MAN   I just find it healthier, I feel better about myself if I…

WOMAN   Does that mean you don't eat pussy or…

MAN   …

WOMAN   Sorry, am I making you uneasy? Sometimes I make people uneasy.

MAN   I just wasn't expecting you to be so…

WOMAN   So you do?

MAN   Well… I have… I can… I… if asked.

WOMAN   That's good of you.

MAN   Thank you.

The pair look at each other. The waiter comes back with a bowl of bread. He looks at the man for quite a while.

MAN   Thank you.

WAITER   Everything alright sir?

MAN   Yes, fine, thank you.

WAITER   OK.

The waiter exits. The conversation becomes strangely sexual.

WOMAN   He's a bit of a *cunt* isn't he?

MAN   ...

WOMAN   Are you a homosexual?

MAN   No.

WOMAN   Ever thought about it?

MAN   No.

WOMAN   So you could be.

MAN   I'm pretty sure I'm not.

WOMAN   Alright.

The woman gets a notepad out of her bag and writes something down.

MAN   What's that?

WOMAN   Just giving you a score.

MAN   Why?

WOMAN   To see what sort of person you are.

MAN   And?

WOMAN   I haven't decided yet.

The woman seductively eats a breadstick

MAN   What... is it you, what's, job, do you have a
                 job?

WOMAN   You don't remember?

MAN   You told me already? I can't…

WOMAN   Possible side effect. Yes, I did.

She scribbles something in her notepad.

MAN   What did you say then?

WOMAN   I said "yes, I did".

MAN   No, before that, you said… you said…

WOMAN   Are you alright Richard?

MAN   I, this, some social situations makes me a
                 bit uncomfortable...

She downs her drink.

WOMAN   Cute

AD AGENCY 3

*A blast of music. An office. The start of the day. Coffees,
suits, warm up routine.*

MAN 1   Morning Gentlemen.

MAN 2, 3   Morning!

MAN 1   Good weekends etc?

MAN 3   Oh here we go.

MAN 1   What?

MAN 2	When you ask us how our weekends were, it's usually because you know that you had a better one.
MAN 1	Well, yes, guilty... Dart board!

Man 2 grabs a felt dart board and hands Man 1 three darts, he throws three darts one after another. Man 2 & 3 react to his score.

MAN 3	Well... Go on
MAN 1	A gentlemen does not kiss and tell...

Man 2 & 3 laugh. He joins in.

MAN 1	Alright, well, we had a few shots in this Soho place, me and this blonde chick, must have been about 22, quite trashy really, tattoos in all the wrong places, but y'know, there's something really sexy about a status fuck.
MAN 3	Lucky prick.
MAN 2	So what happened...?

There is a knock at the door.

MAN 1	Not now Kelly, I'm busy.
KELLY	Well, yes I know, sorry but it's -
MAN 1	Whatever it is it can wait 5 minutes, I'm doing a... briefing.
KELLY	Ok.

He checks she's gone.

MAN 1	...so, I'm with this girl and she's out of her fucking head, it's 3am or something, she's conscious, but y'know, "on the turn".

MAN 3	Mm, medium rare.
MAN 2	What does that mean?
MAN 3	Er, I dunno.
MAN 1	...I bundle her into a cab, get her back to my place and we -

The knock at the door comes again.

MAN 2 & 3	Ohhh!
MAN 1	Busy! Fuck! Are you deaf?
KELLY	Sorry, this can't wait.
MAN 1	Ok, fine, what is it?

Kelly enters.

KELLY	It's Stephen...
MAN 1	Oh fuck off, look if he's claiming unfair dismissal, then he can speak to legal because that man was clearly not fit for the job.
KELLY	His wife found him in their living room this morning, he's dead.
MAN 1	What?
KELLY	Suicide, most likely. The press are sniffing around downstairs, you better get thinking up a pretty good statement... oh and the costume, the costume's causing quite a stir on Twitter, they might want to talk about that... I'll tell them you're on your way...

Pause. She exits.

MAN 1	Fuck!

VERBATIM 2

ACTOR 1   My brain was all I had going for me, and I was failing a lot of my classes. I had no real friends, mum and I fought a lot, and with the added pressure to get straight A's I guess I just sort of snapped. One night before a physics exam I carved the word ZERO into my arm, and I've been self-harming ever since.

ACTOR 2   I was violently raped, 3 days after I arrived for university in a new town. I stopped eating, stopped washing, stopped getting dressed, stopped caring. Eventually I went to the doctor to discuss the crippling insomnia keeping me up 'til four every night, and he immediately pointed out the thing I had failed to notice. The depression.

ACTOR 3   I cannot comprehend how or why anyone would care or be interested in me, I withdraw from the world and switch off my phone, I hurt myself, burning my hands and arms.

ACTOR 4   It's seen as a flaw, a weakness, people don't understand it, people are scared of what they can't see.

GIRLS 2

Girl 1 is in a school park with Magic Mike. They are both smoking and watching a video on Mike's phone.

Some muttering and laughing as Girl 2 enters.

GIRL 2   Hey.

GIRL 1 stubs out a the cigarette on the floor

GIRL 1   Oh hey, shit, sorry babe, I...

GIRL 2   Where have you been? I've been calling you, I thought we were meeting at 5?

GIRL 1   Yeah, I got... held up with -

GIRL 2   - ok, you could've text me, we always meet at -

GIRL 1   I, I must have..Oh, you know Mike right?

GIRL 2   Yeah, I've heard.

MIKE   Alright?

Pause.

GIRL 2   ...So, you, smoke now do you?

GIRL 1   Um...

MIKE   Looks like it...

GIRL 2   Rough.

Mike laughs

MIKE   Sorry Miss, she won't do it again.

GIRL 1   Mike...

GIRL 2 sniffs.

GIRL 2   Can someone smell Dairylea?

GIRL 1 tries not to laugh

MIKE   What?

GIRL 2   Nothing, sorry.

A moment of looking.

GIRL 2   So, are you coming?

GIRL 1   I..

MIKE   Nah, she ain't.

GIRL 2   Well, we had plans, didn't we?

MIKE   Yeah, you *had* plans, but now you don't, she'll catch up later yeah? You see her every fucking day, chill.

GIRL 2   Yeah, she's my best... she's my mate.

GIRL 1   Look, I'll give you a call tonight, ok?

GIRL 2   Whenever you can fit me in would be great...

GIRL 1   Stace...

MIKE   Nice meeting ya.

A look between the two girls. Girl 2 goes to exit.

MIKE   Smoke?

GIRL 2 turns to see GIRL 1 accept a cigarette.

GIRL 1   You shouldn't do that, it'll kill you.

MIKE   Oh, and gashing your stomach open won't?

He chuckles. Silence.

GIRL 2   You... you told him?

GIRL 1   No, look, it's not like that, I -

GIRL 2   Just leave me alone

GIRL 2 runs off. GIRL 1 goes to run after her.

GIRL 1   Stace... Stacey wait.

The girls exit, as the rest of the cast file on to the stage.

ARE YOU OK?

Street sounds. Traffic, conversation etc.

We see the woman from the MAN & WOMAN scene walking the streets, she is clearly distressed.

MAN 1	Are you ok?
WOMAN	Yeah, thanks.
GIRL 1	Everything alright darling?
WOMAN	Yes, fine, thank you.
MAN 2	Cheer up love, might never happen, haha.
WOMAN	I'm fine, I'm… ok.
MAN 3	One of those days eh?
WOMAN	Sorry?
HUSBAND	Change your fucking life.
TEENAGER	Whoa, what happened to you?
GIRL 2	You should get some sleep babe, you look like shit.
WOMAN	I…I…
MAN 5	Give us a smile, it can't be that bad.
GIRL	Mum?

She takes a deep breath, the noises grow, flashes of the car accident again. She pops a pill. The crowd disappear. She is alone with her thoughts for a few moments.

DRESS REHEARSAL

We see GIRL & GUY from the opening scene. The scene is actually a dress rehearsal of a play. They have been renamed THE ACTRESS & MARTIN for this scene.

THE ACTRESS So...what? Fuck buddies?

MARTIN Huh?

THE ACTRESS We can't avoid this forever.

MARTIN No, I know.

Pause. Guy has missed a line. Girl stumbles but continues.

THE ACTRESS What?

MARTIN Er... "Buddy", sounds so American... "Hey buddy, d'you want me to wank you off?"

THE ACTRESS What was that?

MARTIN ...An American.

THE ACTRESS Which American?

MARTIN I don't know, what do you mean? A non-specific one...

The words of the girl go into muffled sound in a voiceover, the Guy's mouth is moving but not much is coming out. We hear sounds of the beach, as if some kind of relaxation technique.

THE ACTRESS Why is a non-specific American offering to wank you off?

MARTIN He's not... it was... Jesus are you always like this?

THE ACTRESS Are you trying to tell me something Mark? You don't want us to be fuck buddies

56

because you'd rather imagine non-specific American men wanking you off?

MARTIN   Fuck off.

THE ACTRESS What's he wanking you off with?

Pause.

THE ACTRESS A donut? That'd be the ultimate American wank wouldn't it?

No response. The sound returns to normal.

THE ACTRESS Wouldn't it?

The guy comes round.

MARTIN   Fuck, yes, sorry. I'm so sorry, where were we?

Pause.

THE ACTRESS "That would be the ultimate American wank…"

The director enters with a script.

DIRECTOR   Ok… guys… this is a DRESS REHEARSAL. Can we just make sure we are all on board with what that means, we open, tomorrow night, this play, that we are currently shitting our way through at the moment, tomorrow, in front of actual people who matter.

THE ACTRESS Sorry, Martin missed a… line, threw me a bit…

MARTIN   Yeah, look, it's my…

DIRECTOR   Is there an issue Martin?

57

He thinks.

MARTIN   No, sorry, I… just didn't have a great night.

DIRECTOR   You know what, right now I don't care, I just want to get through this fucking rehearsal, so Martin if we could just put whatever is going on in there to the back of your mind for the next hour that would be perfect, that would be a dream. "That would be the ultimate American wank wouldn't it?" now let's carry on before we're all fucking dead.

Martin pulls himself together

MARTIN   *[Whispers]* Sorry…

Pause.

THE ACTRESS That would be the ultimate American wank wouldn't it?

Slight pause.

MARTIN   You're weird, you know that?

THE ACTRESS My ex said I was "kookily cuntish".

MARTIN   Nice.

RESTAURANT - PART 2

We see Rich from the restaurant scene. He is sat on a chair, at a desk is Carol, his therapist.

CAROL   So how have things been?

RICH   Um, yeah, OK, I think, better.

CAROL	That's really good Richard, anxiety out of 10, what do you think? Just over the last week.
RICH	A three, four maybe?
CAROL	Well that's amazing, we've come a long way no?
RICH	Yeah.
CAROL	Still having the dreams?
RICH	Yes, pretty intense ones actually.
CAROL	That'll be the medication I'm afraid, they have their pro's and cons as you know, mostly pros in your case I think, they've certainly made a difference, you look a lot more like you, which is, I'm really happy to see that. Sometimes they can linger for a while, but things should start to drop off soon.
RICH	Sorry?
CAROL	The side effects, sorry, tail off, not drop off, that sounds a bit -
RICH	Oh good, yeah, I don't want anything to drop off.
CAROL	Goodness, no, we don't want that.

An awkward laugh and a moment.

CAROL	Right, sorry, so, as you know, this is your last session with me, and anyone I hope, but if you do need anything in the future you can always re-refer yourself to us, you'll have to go through triage and all

that again I'm afraid, guidelines, blah blah blah, but our Emergency number is on the bottom of this letter so, if you ever feel you're in any immediate danger, but, you've got the exercises, and I can see you're in a much better and safer state mentally now so -

RICH I don't want to stop.

CAROL Sorry?

RICH I don't want this to finish, I don't think I'm ready.

CAROL Oh, you are ready Richard, we wouldn't stop if you weren't, I know it's hard when you've had someone to talk to every week, but it's important you don't get dependent on that and that you can manage things by yourself or with someone else.

RICH I don't have anyone else, please.

CAROL Well, you should start to find things get a little easier over time, it won't happen straight away but we got your anxiety down from a 10 when you started therapy, and well, you're a 3 or 4 now, that's great.

RICH I lied, I'm sorry, rip that sheet up please, I'm an 8, I feel like an 8, right now, so, I need -

CAROL I wish I could say to come back next week, I really do, but, we have guidelines in place to ensure we're giving the right amount of treatment and -

RICH   Fuck the guidelines, I just want to talk to
                  you for a bit longer, just one more week,
                  you make me feel happy, you make me feel
                  comfortable and relaxed and -

CAROL   I'm very pleased I've made you feel that
                  way, but It's not uncommon to have
                  feelings for a therapist in this kind of
                  situation, it does happen, it's a very
                  emotionally intense period for the patient,
                  it's called Transference and -

Rich leans in and kisses Carol.

VOICEMAIL   Received today at 11.35am. Hi Richard,
                  it's Carol, just confirming we're meeting at
                  1.30pm tomorrow, if I don't hear
                  otherwise, I'll assume all is well, any
                  problems do give me a call. Bye for now. To
                  listen to the message again... message
                  deleted, you have no new messages.

*Shift to night-time. Richard is on the street, he throws his
phone on the floor.*

RICHARD   SHIT!

GIRLS 3

*Girl 2 is at the top of the ladder. Richard turns and punches
the side of the ladder.*

GIRL 2   Watch it!

He looks up.

RICHARD   Sorry, fuck that really hurt, I didn't see
                  you... otherwise I wouldn't have... what
                  are you doing up there? It's dangerous

61

GIRL 2   What does it look like I'm doing?

RICHARD   Well, it… looks like you're cold, up a ladder… haven't you got a coat?

GIRL 2   …No, I didn't exactly plan this.

RICHARD   Well, that's why you should always have a coat… just in case. Even in the Summer, you never know.

GIRL 2   Right.

RICHARD   But… don't jump.

GIRL 2   Who says I was gonna jump?

RICHARD   You're up a ladder, on your own, with no coat, I assume you're not stargazing.

GIRL 2   No offence, but it's not really any of your business is it?

RICHARD   Ok, fair enough.

Silence.

GIRL 2   Are you still down there?

RICHARD   Yeah, I am.

GIRL 2   Why?

RICHARD   I sort of feel responsible now, you've put me in a very difficult position.

GIRL 2   Fuck off then, I don't need your help.

RICHARD   That's ok, you're upset, I understand, me too, I've had a really fucking, sorry, shit, sorry, day, a bad day, and I just understand, I understand why you're up a ladder with no coat. Well, not the coat bit, but, I've, y'know, I know how you feel.

GIRL 2   I fucking hate it when people say that.

RICHARD   Yeah, sorry, but, well, I just get it.

Silence.

RICHARD   You wouldn't kill yourself though, jumping off there.

GIRL 2   Why?

RICHARD   Well you're not high enough for a start and this is all muddy grass down here, you'd just come crashing down, regret it, and end up breaking an arm or a leg or a rib. The human body is surprisingly tough... it's the mind you've got to watch out for.

GIRL 2   So, I should just find somewhere higher is that what you're saying? Are you giving me tips?

RICHARD   No, God, no no, I'm just saying, it's...

GIRL 2   I'm joking. I wasn't planning on jumping, I just needed to get away for a bit

RICHARD   Why? ...If you don't mind?

GIRL 2   I admitted to my best friend today that I cut myself, and she ran away and told this guy that she sucked off at a party and now thinks she's in love with.

RICHARD   Oh.

GIRL 2   Yeah, exactly, so now she knows, he knows and probably everyone in the fucking school knows, and I just feel stupid.

63

RICHARD	What about your parents, do they…
GIRL 2	Well my Mum's dead, and my Dad drinks until he blacks out, so, I'm kind of dealing with this one on my own.
RICHARD	I'm sorry.

Silence

GIRL 2	It's alright… What are you doing out here anyway? Snooping around at night. In the woods. Bit creepy.
RICHARD	I… I'm not snooping, I, had a relapse, a, well a blip really, I guess, and I thought, I had beaten it, I thought, I'd finally got through it, like everyone always said I would but, I realised that I'd become dependent on her… my fucking therapist, and I had this image in my head, this fantasy that she'd fallen for me, I know, it's stupid and I, I kissed her.
GIRL 2	Shit.
RICHARD	I just thought, at that moment, it would make me happy and… and… I realised she hadn't, she hadn't fallen for me. Of course she hadn't, she was, just doing her job. So, I ran away, I'm 40 years old, and I ran away because I couldn't deal with it, I tried to kiss a woman and she didn't want to kiss me back. And, I realised, that nobody wants me, because, because I'm like this, all the time, and I don't know how to… I don't know what to do -

The girl comes down a couple of steps of the ladder. She drops down a bottle of water.

GIRL 2   ...help yourself.

RICHARD   Thanks.

He takes a gulp, then spits it out

RICHARD   God, what's that?

GIRL 2   Vodka.

RICHARD   Vodka? You're what like sixteen?

GIRL 2   Fifteen actually, I'm very mature for my age.

RICHARD   Well, you shouldn't be drinking.

GIRL 2   And you shouldn't be hanging out in parks with 15 year old's.

RICHARD   We're not "hanging out" I...

GIRL 2   Joke

She starts to climb down the steps.

RICHARD   Well, I'm glad you weren't going to kill yourself.

GIRL 2   Yeah, me too... I think.

He hands her back the bottle.

GIRL 2   Thanks.

RICHARD   You'll be ok will you?

<u>IN MY HEAD</u>

A television studio. 25 years in the future.

65

A glittery curtain appears. Signs (projection or physical) read "IN MY HEAD". Lights flash. Game show music. Loud, excitable applause. Behind the three boxes, are three emaciated looking contestants in drab clothing. Out front is the presenter in a glittery jacket, slick hair and painted on showbiz grin.

PRESENTER   Well hello, hello, hello, hello! Welcome back to part 2 of IN. MY. HEAD and If you've just joined us -

He gestures to the audience as if awaiting a catchphrase.

AUDIENCE   Where. Have. You. Been?!

The audience laugh and applaud

PRESENTER   Couldn't have said it better myself. So, here we are, the show that everyone is talking about, we put three members of the public with mental health conditions up against each other to win a VERY SPECIAL PRIZE.

Audience applause and oohs.

PRESENTER   And let's have a reminder for the lovely people at home what today's prize is.

VOICEOVER   That's right, today's special prize is an 8 week CBT course for you AND a friend, made possible by the lovely people at the World Health Service.

Audience applause

PRESENTER   Just look at their desperate faces, what. A. prize, worth a total of £20,000.

Audience applause

PRESENTER   This is going to be some show, I can feel it. So contestant number 1, what would that prize mean to you?

CONTESTANT 1 I... would... it would... I would be able to get my life back on track.

Sympathetic applause and "awws".

PRESENTER   Ah, well ain't that the best, good luck, good luck contestant number 1, and to the rest of you, let's crack straight on and play ROUND 2.

Some flashing lights. Projection: ROUND 2 flashes on and off. Some music. Abruptly stops.

PRESENTER   Round two is called, FACE THE CONDITION, we will show you lots and lots of faces from the past, all, just like you three here, suffering from a broken brain and all we need you to do is buzz in when you spot the person with the condition we're looking for. And today's condition is.. BI-POLAR DISORDER.

Audience applause and cheers.

PRESENTER   Oh that's a tricky one! Just buzz in when you think you see it, and remember, you are playing for your mental wellbeing here, so, pay. close. attention. Let's play in 3... 2... 1. Show us the faces.

Some game show music. A load of Facebook style profile pictures appear flashing up one at a time on the screen. The contestants look out, the images appear behind them.

After a while someone buzzes in. An incorrect noise plays

PRESENTER   Oh, I'm afraid not contestant number 2, that was in fact... sadness. She was just sad, easy mistake to make, we've all done it but I'm afraid that means you are frozen out. Let's play on!

More faces, slightly faster this time

PRESENTER   Keep watching, they're in there somewhere.

Contestant 3 buzzes in.

PRESENTER   No, no, afraid not, that one was just tired, and being sleepy isn't a mental illness, if it was we'd all be on this show.

Audience laughter

PRESENTER   Haha, ok, contestant number 3 is frozen out, and 1 and 2, you're now in play. So, keep those eyes peeled.

The images flash up for a third time. After a while contestant number 2 buzzes in. Flashing lights and a "jackpot" style sound effect. Audience applause.

PRESENTER   Yes, congratulations, contestant number 2, the points are yours.

Audience applause

PRESENTER   I wasn't lying when I said it was a tricky one huh? Ok, so as the points stand, Contestant number 1 has -

VOICEOVER   100 points.

PRESENTER   Contestant number 2 has -

VOICEOVER   300 points.

PRESENTER And Contestant number 3 has -

VOICEOVER 200 points.

PRESENTER Not much in it eh folks? Not much at all, can you feel the tension rising in the studio? Exciting isn't it? Now before we carry on let's quickly talk to you Contestant number 3, now this is an interesting story, you used to be a teacher is that right?

CONTESTANT 3 I did yes.

PRESENTER But something happened didn't it?

CONTESTANT 3 I, was fired, because, my condition, they didn't think it was appropriate for children to be taught by someone who was... mentally unstable.

PRESENTER Wow, did you hear that folks? What a crazy society we live in, but, hey look for the positive, you're on the television. If they're watching, those, people at your school, watching you right now, is there anything you'd like to say?

CONTESTANT 3 Yeah, fuck you, you animals.

PRESENTER Whoa, whoa, ok, ok, when I said anything... sorry about that folks, a little rude word slipped through the net there, would you mind apologising for that bit of language to the lovely people at home?

CONTESTANT 3 Why should I apologise, it's your show?

A security guy steps out of the shadows, carrying a taser

PRESENTER   Ha, because it's 8pm on a Monday evening darling and if you need that therapy, which, we all know you do, I suggest say you say it, or our friend here throws you back out on the street. Your choice.

Pause.

CONTESTANT 3 I'm... sorry

PRESENTER   There we go, now everyone's happy

The audience applauds. The security man backs away.

PRESENTER   Ok, so, on with the show. It's time to eliminate one contestant in this next round which we call ATTENTION SEEKERS. Now we all know that people with a mental condition love attention right?

AUDIENCE   Right!

PRESENTER   So now, contestant's the spotlight is well and truly on you.

The lighting changes dramatically

AUDIENCE   Oooh!

PRESENTER   You want the prize? Well please our eyes. It's time to win over the audience with your best dance moves, magical smiles (if you remember how) and well, we'll leave the rest up to your imaginations. We'll go by audience reaction so, if you're ready, when the music kicks in, it's time, to -

AUDIENCE   SEEK. THAT. ATTENTION.

Applause.

Some loud, bassy music kicks in. The three contestants all move in slow mo, they look uncomfortable but are trying their best to win over the audience, we hear the sounds of slow mo, distorted cheers of an audience.

Every so often the scene will speed up as a projection appears on the wall "WORK IT!" "TRY HARDER" "STRIP! STRIP!" "COME ON!" etc. And then back to slow mo.

The noise builds and builds everything gets more frantic and sinister and suddenly drowns into an echo.

GRADUATES

Outside. Noises of distant traffic. The group are drinking and smoking.

GUY 1   That was a fucking sweet night.

GUY 2   Bloody lovely night mate.

GIRL   I threw up on my ex during the slow dance, fuck.

GUY 1   Yeah that was quality.

GUY 2   Yep, properly funny, I mean *well done.*

GIRL   I'm so embarrassed.

GUY 1   You're rich, you don't get embarrassed.

GIRL   No, I'm not rich, my parents are.

GUY 1   Yeah, exactly, so, you're just like...*delayed* rich

GUY 2   Want me to go round with a spade and bash them in?

The guys laughs.

71

GUY 1	That's a bit fucking dark mate, chill out.
GUY 2	It was a joke, it was only a joke Sally, I wouldn't really bash them in... I think they're both lovely people for the record.
GIRL	Oh good, well I'm glad my parents will survive the night.

Silence.

GUY 3	So... are we all ready for it then?
GUY 1	What's that mate?
GUY 3	Life, are we ready for it?

They all laugh

GUY 2	Alright Attenborough, calm down.
GUY 1	Attenborough does animals mate.
GUY 3	Yeah well animals are life aren't they mate?
GIRL	When did you get so philosophical exactly Richard?
GUY 2	I think that might have been about the time that Damo gave him that spliff.
GUY 3	I use this to relax actually, it really helps, I always think about this kind of thing.
GUY 2	Yeah, cut to 10 years later and he's a crazy loner fucking talking to himself.
GIRL	Come on guys.
GUY 2	I'm fucking starving, could murder a panini.
GUY 1	The thinking man's kebab.

GUY 2	Bloody hell.
GIRL	I think we'll all have a pretty good life actually. Just think, this is the best time that there's ever been to be alive.
GUY 1	Yeah, not sure I'd agree with you there.
GUY 2	Ditto.
GIRL	Ok, logic being?
GUY 2	Hello! Syria, Rolf Harris. That's all life is at the moment, fucking death and celebrity nonces. It's bleak.
GIRL	Ok, do we really need to be having this conversation now?
GUY 2	You started it.
GIRL	Actually he started it with his... fucking... life thing.
GUY 3	Look, I'm just saying, that we, this won't get any easier, we won't get this moment again, our lives from now on are going to change massively, and not just because we've left uni and we're out in the big wide world, I mean, fucking, the planet, who knows what's going to happen.
GUY 2	David Attenborough?
They laugh.	
GUY 3	No, I'm serious, I mean, the scientists, they monitor this stuff supposedly, they know what's going on, the government, they certainly do, and do you think they'd tell us? Do you think they'd tell us the little

people if something was wrong? We could be on the brink of fucking extinction, our skin peeling from our faces, while they're all down in the bunker, living it up.

GIRL   Can we not talk about this, it's depressing.

GUY 2   She's got a point mate. Skin peeling from our faces? Fucking hell.

GUY 3   Sorry, I'm not making it up, I'm not trying to be depressing, the fact is life is depressing, y'know, we're told to go out and earn money, and get a job as soon as we can except there aren't any, and build a future, for what? There's so much fucking radiation flying through our heads 24/7 I'd be amazed if we even make it to 40. People don't just kill themselves for a laugh you know? It takes a really strong fucking person to be able to just get through the day without breaking down at the end of it. A quarter of people with a mental health condition, I mean, should we be surprised? And you know the sad part, most of them, probably don't even realise, they just think that's how everyone feels, they just accept it and struggle on.

Beat.

GUY 3   I just feel, so, helpless sometimes y'know, I just store everything up and then, it just has to come flooding out.

GUY 2   It's alright mate.

GIRL   Yeah, you've got us.

GUY 1	Yeah, you big fucking mental.
GIRL	Dan!
GUY 1	Sorry, I thought I'd use humour to disperse the tension
GUY 3	No, no, you're right, sorry guys, it's, fuck, it's just all so overwhelming sometimes you know?
GUY 2	Yeah, no, I totally get that mate, I feel like that sometimes, like, when I get a really big hangover, and I just think, this is it, this is the end of the road, I'm a fucking gonner, and then I just have some green tea, take some deep breaths, put on some Big Bang Theory, sorted.
GIRL	Green tea and deep breaths?
GUY 2	Fuck off, we've all got our methods.
GUY 3	Thanks, it's, I don't know what I'd do if you lot weren't around.
GUY 1	Have a wank?

They laugh.

GUY 1   Nah, joking mate, we'll all look out for each other yeah? In this big scary world.

He hugs Guy 2 in a manly way for too long. Pause.

GIRL   Right, well I think, after all that, what we need... is a photo!

She pulls out her iPhone on the end of a Selfie stick.

GUY 1   Oh the fucking selfie stick's out. You want a bleak vision of the future mate, right there.

GIRL   It's just a bit of fun.

They groan.

GIRL   Look, are we doing this or not?

GUY 2   Ok! Come on guys, best smiles!

They all arrange into a photo.

GUY 3   Oh god... I hate this.

GIRL   Let's just, remember being happy. Three, Two, One –

They all pull faces. Guy 3 is doing a painted on smile. The image freezes, there is a big flash and iPhone camera sound, the image then appears as a projection on the back wall then fades.

VERBATIM 3

ACTOR 1   I don't see a therapist anymore and feel I have been coping okay on my own. I've lived abroad, I run a charity, I've moved cities to start a new job, I'm successful at work, I have lots of friends, I have a good family relationship... but I do still have some problems.

ACTOR 2   I took up exercise, which actually helps immeasurably, and I moved to a significantly less stressful job to give myself time to recover.

ACTOR 3   There was a lot of suffering for many years until I got on the right meds. Now that I finally have the right treatment the suffering is greatly reduced. But that was 20 years of suffering.

ACTOR 4   I saw a psychotherapist for 3 years, I'm now married to a wonderful man, have some great friends and have a job that I love and that I am successful at. Some days I still struggle but most days I win the battle.

ACTOR 5   I turned to self-help CBT, Self-taught mindfulness, exercise and healthy eating. I've only had one panic attack in the past year and my mood is far more optimistic and stable.

ACTOR 6   Being *cured* isn't the answer, my condition is with me for life, I still have trouble resisting the blades on bad days.

Pause.

CRAZY

Actor 6 sings.

ACTOR 6   Does that make me crazy?

Does that make me crazy?

Does that make me crazy? Probably...

The Company Sings. The piece should be arranged a capella to the loose tune of Gnarls Barkley 'Crazy'.

CAST   I remember when,

I remember, I remember when I lost my mind

There was something so special about that place

Even your emotions have an echo, in so much space

And when you're out there, without care

Yeah you were out of touch

But it wasn't because I didn't know enough

I just knew too much

Does that make me crazy?

Does that make me crazy?

Does that make me crazy?

Possibly...

The voices build, the final note lingers, then silence.

Blackout.

End.